Modern Industrial World

Australia

David Lowe and Andrea Shimmen

RSVP

RAINTREE
STECK-VAUGHN
PUBLISHERS

The Steck-Vaughn Company

Austin, Texas

MODERN INDUSTRIAL WORLD

Australia   **Portugal**
Canada   **Russia**
France   **South Africa**
Germany   **Spain**
Japan   **Sweden**

2901

Cover: The Gold Coast, Queensland
Title page: Visitors climbing Uluru, one of Australia's most spectacular rocks
Contents page: Aboriginal dancers at sunset

© **Copyright 1997, text, Steck-Vaughn Company**

Published by Raintree Steck-Vaughn Publishers,
an imprint of Steck-Vaughn Company

Library of Congress Cataloging-in-Publication Data
Lowe, David.
Australia / David Lowe and Andrea Shimmen.
    p.   cm.—(Modern industrial world)
    Includes bibliographical references and index.
    Summary: Surveys the geography, history, natural resources, peoples and cultures, economy, and government of the sixth-biggest country in the world.
    ISBN 0-8172-4553-7
    1. Australia—Juvenile literature.
    2. Australia—Description and travel—Juvenile literature.
    3. Australia—Economic conditions—1945—Juvenile literature.
    [1. Australia.]
    I. Shimmen, Andrea. II. Title. III. Series.
    DU96.L69   1996
    919.4—dc20   95-42669

Printed in Italy
1 2 3 4 5 6 7 8 9 0 01 00 99 98 97

Contents

Introduction	4
The Island Continent	6
History	12
Peoples of Australia	18
Cities	24
Harvests of Land and Sea	28
Manufacturing and Services	34
Daily Life	40
The Future	44
Glossary	46
Further Information	47
Index	48

Introduction

Australia is a country that has changed and developed at a great pace, especially since World War II. The population of the country is still fairly small, but it is one of the most diverse in the world. Australians are proud that their nation includes Aboriginal, European, Asian, Pacific, and other settlers.

Visitors and immigrants come to Australia for a number of reasons: the open spaces, the natural beauty of the countryside and beaches, the sports and outdoor lifestyle, and the high standard of living. They also come to start businesses and to enjoy Australia's rich culture.

Above Most Australians live in or around cities. This is a busy street in Sydney.

Left A surfer off the Gold Coast. Surfing is one of the many popular outdoor sports in Australia.

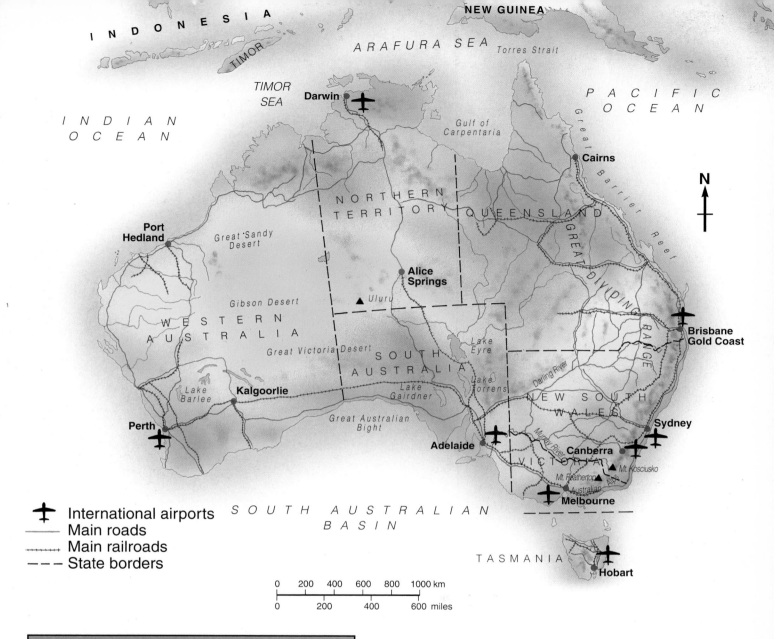

NEW GUINEA

INDONESIA

ARAFURA SEA Torres Strait

TIMOR

TIMOR SEA

Darwin

INDIAN OCEAN

PACIFIC OCEAN

Gulf of Carpentaria

Cairns

N

N O R T H E R N
T E R R I T O R Y

Q U E E N S L A N D

GREAT DIVIDING RANGE

Great Barrier Reef

Port Hedland

Great Sandy Desert

Gibson Desert

W E S T E R N
A U S T R A L I A

Great Victoria Desert

Alice Springs

▲ Uluru

S O U T H
A U S T R A L I A

Lake Eyre

Brisbane Gold Coast

Lake Torrens

Darling River

N E W   S O U T H
W A L E S

Lake Barlee

Kalgoorlie

Lake Gairdner

Murray River

Sydney

Perth

Great Australian Bight

Adelaide

Canberra

V I C T O R I A

Mt. Feathertop ▲ Mt. Kosciusko
Australian

Melbourne

✈ International airports
— Main roads
┅ Main railroads
- - - State borders

S O U T H   A U S T R A L I A N
B A S I N

T A S M A N I A

Hobart

0   200   400   600   800   1000 km
0   200   400   600 miles

AUSTRALIA AT A GLANCE

Area:	2,967,909 square miles
Population (1995):	18 million
Population density:	6 people per square mile
Capital:	Canberra
Languages:	English; languages belonging to different communities
Currency:	Australian dollar

Movies made in Australia, such as *The Road Warrior*, *The Piano*, and *Muriel's Wedding*, have been seen in many countries. Australian art, ballet, and opera are also well known overseas, and authors such as Thomas Keneally and Peter Carey have won international awards for their work.

Many people know Australians for their strength in sports such as rugby and swimming. In A.D. 2000, when Sydney hosts the Olympic Games, Australia's sporting reputation will be on display to the world.

5

The Island Continent

Uluru stands out strikingly against the flat surrounding landscape.

Australia is a huge island, and the sixth biggest country in the world. It is separated from its neighbors by sea. New Zealand lies to the southeast, but most of Australia's neighbors are to the north. The closest are Papua New Guinea and the islands of Indonesia. The nearest part of Indonesia, Irian Jaya (the western half of New Guinea), is less than two hundred miles from the northern tip of Australia. To the west and south of Australia lies the vast Indian Ocean, and beyond the Indian Ocean to the south is the Antarctic Ocean and Antarctica.

DIMENSIONS

The size of Australia as compared with Europe, the United States, Brazil, and India:

Europe	3,997,929 square miles
United States	3,615,123 square miles
Brazil	3,284,426 square miles
Australia	2,967,909 square miles
India	1,229,424 square miles

Source: *Webster's New Geographical Dictionary*

Australia's area becomes even bigger if we include its seven external territories. Australia is responsible for administering a number of small island territories, including Norfolk Island, the Cocos (Keeling) Islands, and Christmas Island. By far the biggest is Australia's Antarctic Territory, which covers 2.5 million square miles.

Australia covers three different time zones. Sydney on the east coast is two hours ahead of Perth on the west coast.

Average maximum temperature in January (in °F)

- Above 102°
- 97–102°
- 91–97°
- 81–91°
- 75–81°
- 70–75°
- Under 70°

Average minimum temperature in July (in °F)

- Above 54°
- 48–54°
- 43–48°
- 37–43°
- 32–37°
- Under 0°

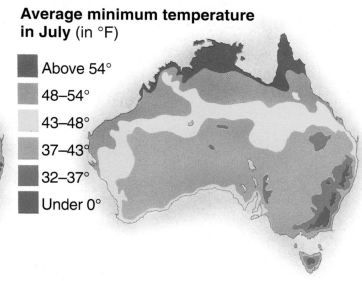

Average number of rain days per year (when daily rainfall of at least 0.01 inch of rain is recorded)

- Over 200
- 160-200
- 120-160
- 80-120
- 40-80
- 20-40
- Under 20

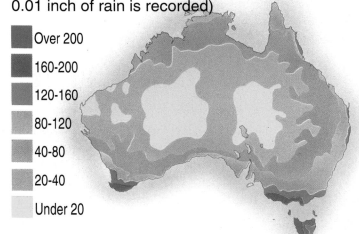

RAINFALL IN AUSTRALIAN CITIES		
	RAINFALL (inches)	
CITY	Jan.	July
Adelaide	0.8	2.6
Alice Springs	1.5	0.67
Brisbane	16.7	1.1
Cairns	16.7	1.1
Canberra	2.4	1.5
Darwin	16.4	0.04
Hobart	1.9	2.0
Melbourne	1.8	1.9
Perth	0.31	6.9
Sydney	4.0	3.9

Source: *Australian Bureau of Meteorology, 1989*

WEATHER AND CLIMATE

Most of Australia is hot and dry, but there are great differences between regions. The main difference in the weather is between the north and south. Almost a third of northern Australia is in the tropics. Therefore, northern Australia has higher average temperatures than the southern half of the continent. Much of northwestern Australia has a summer average temperature of about 95°F. The north has heavy monsoon rains in summer and occasional tropical cyclones that can cause great damage. Tropical cyclone Tracy, which struck Darwin

on Christmas Day, 1974, destroyed more than half the buildings in the city and killed 50 people.

Southern Australia receives most of its rainfall in winter. The coastal areas of the south and southeast, where most of the population lives, have milder weather. Tasmania, the most southern state, has the coolest climate.

The capital cities in the southeast corner of the mainland —Adelaide, Melbourne, and Sydney—often have hot summers. Strong northerly winds combine with high temperatures, causing bushfires to break out in surrounding forests. In recent years such fires have burned large areas of forest and pasture close to these cities.

Bushfires, like this one, often break out in Australia because of the hot, dry summer conditions.

OLD AND DRY CONTINENT

Some of Australia's rocks are more than three billion years old and are spectacular features of the Australian landscape. Uluru (formerly Ayers Rock) in central Australia is the best known rock and is one of the most sacred places for the Yankuntjatjara and Pitjantjatjara Aboriginal people.

This tropical rain forest in northeast Queensland receives heavy rainfall.

This group of rocks in Australia's Northern Territory is called the Olgas. They could be more than three billion years old.

Apart from Antarctica, Australia is the driest continent. Uluru sits in the middle of a vast expanse of desert. Almost three-quarters of Australia is arid or semiarid, and the deserts range from rocky plains to fine sand and spinifex grass. The town of Alice Springs, 280 miles to the northeast of Uluru, averages about 11 inches of rainfall each year. Droughts are common, and farmers in parts of Queensland, New South Wales, and Victoria have all received emergency aid from the government to help fight drought in the 1990s.

Closer to the coastline, the picture changes. In northeast Queensland, the tropical rain forest is soaked by high rainfall. It supports an amazing variety of plants and animals within a small area. Farther south, in the southern parts of Victoria and Tasmania, high rainfall allows for more rain forests. Off the northeast coast lies the Great Barrier Reef. Stretching for 1,250 miles, it is the largest coral reef in the world and is home to more than 1,500 species of fish.

MOUNTAINS

Australia is the lowest, flattest continent. Much of the desert interior is just above sea level. Most of Australia's highest ground is found in the Great Dividing Range, a long strip of mountains that runs the length of the east coast. In the southeast corner of the country are the Australian Alps, the country's highest mountains and part of the Great Dividing Range. Mount Kosciusko (named by a Polish explorer after Tadeusz Kosciuszko, a Polish patriot and a hero of the American Revolution) is the highest in the range at 7,310 feet.

Mount Feathertop, in the Great Dividing Range. In some winters, the snowfall in the Australian Alps covers a greater area than the snowfall in the Swiss Alps.

WATER AND RIVERS

The most important Australian rivers are the Murray and the Darling, which drain water from much of the Great Dividing Range. The Murray-Darling system has a catchment of 424,000 square miles. Most of Australia's irrigated land can be found here.

Underground water from the Great Artesian Basin is essential for many inhabitants in central Australia. This reservoir of water lies beneath almost a quarter of the continent.

Research into the management of Australia's water resources has become very important. Increased salinity of water tables and high levels of evaporation are two of the biggest water problems.

WORLD HERITAGE

The World Heritage Committee (set up by UNESCO in the 1970s) aims to protect places that have outstanding universal value and form part of a country's cultural and natural heritage. In 1993, there were 378 places on the World Heritage list. Australia now has twelve areas on this list, including the Great Barrier Reef and Uluru National Park. Farming and tourism can continue in World Heritage areas, but laws prevent any activity that is likely to damage the special characteristics of the area. Acceptance of the Tasmanian Wilderness area as a World Heritage area in 1988 stopped construction of a dam on the Franklin River. The issue of this dam had caused angry battles between conservationists and local workers.

The Murray River winds its way through the Great Dividing Range.

World Heritage Areas
1 Kakadu National Park
2 Wet tropics of Queensland
3 Riversleigh fossil site
4 Great Barrier Reef
5 Uluru National Park
6 Shark Bay
7 Fraser Island
8 Australian Rain Forest Parks
9 Willandra Lakes
10 Lord Howe Island
11 Victoria fossil cave
12 Tasmanian Wilderness

History

THE ABORIGINES

Australia's first people were the Aborigines. They have occupied the continent for more than 40,000 years. Before European settlement in 1788 their population was probably 300,000.

For at least one hundred years before European settlement, northern Australia was visited by fishermen from islands to Australia's north. Today, some of these people, the Macassans, still sail south to Australia to collect trepang, or sea cucumber, from coastal waters.

Above White settlers fighting with the Aborigines. When the white settlers arrived in Australia, some Aborigines fought to keep them off their land.

EUROPEANS

Dutch sailors explored most of the north, west, and south coasts of Australia during the seventeenth century. The Portuguese may have mapped the east coast a century before. But the best known explorer of the east coast was English captain James Cook. He sailed the length of this coast in 1770. His reports led to the British settlement of Australia.

The British settlement of Australia began in 1788, when the First Fleet brought 1,500 people from England, nearly half of whom were convicts. Captain Cook had called the area where he had landed New South Wales. Historians still argue about why the British settled in Australia. Some say that Great Britain was trying to find new places to send convicts because the British prisons were too crowded. Others claim that the British wanted to use Australia's timber and flax (flax was used for making ropes and sails) or wanted to prevent other Europeans from claiming Australia as theirs.

Captain James Cook, the famous explorer of the east coast of Australia

EXPANSION IN THE NINETEENTH CENTURY

Australia's white population grew slowly in the first forty years after 1788. Most of the people were either convicts or former convicts who had finished their sentences. In 1827, Great Britain claimed Australia as its own. From this time, new areas along the coastline were settled, more immigrants arrived from Great Britain, and sheep farming developed. Great Britain provided much of the money for the farms and settlements and bought Australian wool. New colonies called Victoria, Western Australia, Tasmania, and Queensland were established. They later became States of the Commonwealth of Australia.

It was the discovery of gold in several of the colonies in the 1850s that caused a great increase in the Australian population. In 1851, there were less than half a million Australians. Ten years later, there were more than 1.1 million.

The second half of the nineteenth century was an era of expansion and urbanization. Gold, wool, and railroads enabled Australians to spread inland from the coasts or to settle in growing cities such as Sydney and Melbourne. For many Aboriginal tribes it was an era of running away or dying, as the whites refused to share land with people they considered inferior or even subhuman.

Men panning for gold. In the 1850s, thousands of people from all over the world came to Australia to look for gold and try to make their fortunes.

DEVELOPMENT

Stanley Melbourne Bruce, an Australian prime minister in the 1920s, said that what Australia needed was "men, money, and markets." Many other Australian politicians before and after him agreed. For more than sixty years after federation in 1901, Australia's future was closely tied to Great Britain. From Great Britain would come more workers to develop industries, investment for new projects, and agreements to buy most of Australia's wool, meat, fruit, and grain crops.

Great Britain provided these things for Australia until World War II (1939–45), but Australian industry developed slowly. The need to produce munitions for fighting a war in the Pacific meant that Australian industry had to expand. After 1945, it grew more quickly, helped by the arrival of new immigrants. Australia now took continental European as well as British immigrants, and the population increased more quickly. American investment in Australia also became important.

In the 1960s, Australians began mining and exporting large amounts of iron ore, coal, bauxite, and nickel. Japan took many of these new exports, and since then Japan and other east Asian countries have been important trading partners for Australia. Some people have said, "If the Japanese economy sneezes, Australia catches a cold."

Australian Politics since 1901

THE COMMONWEALTH OF AUSTRALIA

The six Australian colonies, New South Wales, Victoria, Western Australia, Tasmania, Queensland, and South Australia, joined as states within the new Commonwealth of Australia in 1901. This process is called federation. There have been no political revolutions and no great changes in the rules of Australian politics since 1901.

Today, Australians have their laws and rules set by the Australian Government in Canberra, known as the federal government; by their state government; and by their local government. Australia is a constitutional monarchy. The Queen of Australia, who is also the Queen of England, is Australia's head of state. The Queen plays no role in Australian politics, and she is really just a symbol. She may not be Australia's head of state for much longer, because many Australians favor becoming a republic and choosing their own head of state.

FEDERAL AND STATE GOVERNMENT

The federal government makes most of the laws that affect Australians. In areas such as education, law and order, and health, the state governments play important roles. They have fewer powers now, though, than they had earlier in the century.

Both federal and state governments have Cabinets made up of Ministries. The prime minister is head of the Australian Government, and the state Premiers are the heads of the state governments. The two main parties in Australian politics are the Labor Party and the Liberal Party.

The Australian Prime Minister, Paul Keating. He is the head of the Labor Party, which by 1995 had ruled Australia for twelve consecutive years.

AUSTRALIA IN THE WORLD

Australians' outlook on the world today is very different from earlier this century. Until some time after World War II, most Australians felt that they were both Australian and British at the same time. They also relied on the British Royal Navy for defense.

Australians fought alongside British troops in World War I, and 30,000 Australian soldiers died. When Japanese forces came to the edge of Australia in 1942, it was clear how important U.S. military help would be for Australia. In 1951, Australia, New Zealand, and the United States signed a security treaty known as ANZUS, which is still very important to the Australian Government.

Legally, Australia became independent from Great Britain in 1931, but very few Australians wanted to feel independent until over thirty years later. Today, Australians feel very independent and know that their main concerns overseas are more with Asia and the Pacific than with Europe.

Australian soldiers in the Pacific Ocean during World War II. Australians also fought in Europe and in the Middle East.

SNOWY MOUNTAINS SCHEME

One huge project that began soon after World War II was the Snowy Mountains Scheme, a dam on the border between Victoria and New South Wales. Today the dam catches millions of tons of water that is used to generate electricity and also to irrigate the dry land farther west. It took 25 years to build the Snowy Mountains Scheme, and many of the workers were newly arrived immigrants from Europe.

The Snowy Mountains, one of the wettest areas in Australia

AUSTRALIA SINCE THE 1980s

Australian governments of the 1980s made sweeping changes to Australia's economy. Up to that time, the Australian economy had relied heavily on a narrow range of exports. Governments had been reluctant to allow too much foreign influence over Australian business and working conditions. In the 1980s this situation changed quickly. The value of the Australian dollar was changing constantly, banking regulations were removed, higher levels of foreign investment were welcomed, public enterprises were privatized, and Australia committed itself to reducing its protection of local industries.

An Asian businesswoman. Since the 1980s, Australia has been doing more business with Asia.

These were the biggest changes in Australia's economic life this century, and they caused some uncertainty and a great deal of debate. Australian politics since the 1980s has been largely a case of the political parties offering ways to make these changes work to Australia's advantage, without causing too much hardship to workers.

> *"The great turnaround in contemporary Australian history is that the region from which we sought in the past to protect ourselves…is now the region which offers Australia the most. Our future lies, inevitably, in the Asia-Pacific region. This is where we live, must survive strategically and economically, and find a place and role if we are to develop our full potential as a nation."* **—Gareth Evans (Australian Foreign Minister) and Bruce Grant,** *Australia's Foreign Relations in the World of the 1990s,* **1992**

Peoples of Australia

The Aborigines were the first Australians. They have a much smaller population now than they had at the time of European settlement, because many were either killed by the new settlers or died from the new illnesses that the settlers had brought to Australia.

Since European settlement in 1788, nearly five million people from almost two hundred countries have immigrated to Australia. Until the end of World War II in 1945, almost all of these immigrants were from Great Britain and Ireland. Immediately after the war many eastern Europeans who no longer had homes (refugees) settled in Australia. In the 1950s, many of the people settling in Australia were from southern Europe. More recently, larger numbers of people from southeast Asia have made Australia their home.

Australia's population today is over 18 million. This is more than double the population of 50 years ago, but it is still small for a country of its size. In recent years, the population growth has slowed down because fewer immigrants have entered Australia.

The ancestors of these Aboriginal children were the first people in Australia.

POPULATION DENSITY (1995)		
	Area in square miles	People per square mile
Australia	2,966,200	6
Bangladesh	57,295	2,184
Brazil	3,284,426	48
Canada	3,851,809	7
Denmark	16,629	311
Great Britain	93,598	616
New Zealand	103,736	32
Sweden	173,665	50
United States	3,615,123	69

Source: *The World Almanac, 1995*

ABORIGINES AND TORRES STRAIT ISLANDERS

In 1921, there were only 61,000 Aborigines and Torres Strait Islanders in Australia. By 1991, this had increased to 270,000—1.5 percent of the Australian population. Aboriginal people have had greater health and housing problems than the average Australian and poorer educational and employment opportunities. Also, access to the political and legal systems had been limited because Aborigines were not allowed to vote in national elections until 1967.

Aborigines today are a diverse group. About half the population lives in country towns, 28 percent lives in the capital cities, and 20 percent lives in more remote parts of the country. They participate in all areas of Australian society. There are still many problems, but government programs to improve the health of children have been fairly successful. During the 1970s and 1980s, new laws enabled Aboriginal people to have more control over their land, and the Aboriginal and Torres Strait Islander Commission, formed in 1990, has given the Aboriginal people more chance to make decisions on other issues concerning their communities. An important decision in the High Court of Australia in 1992, known as the Mabo judgment, recognized Aborigines' rights to traditional lands. When the British arrived in 1788, Australia was considered to be *terra nullius,* or a land with no owners.

Legislation dealing with the Mabo decision, called the Native Title Act, balances the interests of Aborigines, miners, and farmers. It will help compensate the Aborigines for land taken from them by settlers.

Cathy Freeman, an Aboriginal athlete, at the Commonwealth Games in 1994. She is holding the Aboriginal flag, a recognized symbol of the Aborigines.

IMMIGRANTS

The only other country to have had a bigger immigration program than Australia since 1945 is Israel. Four out of ten Australians today were born overseas or had a parent born overseas. Most of these immigrants have settled in the two largest cities, Sydney and Melbourne.

In general, Australians have welcomed the large numbers of immigrants to the country, but there has been some tension. A few people were concerned about the high level of Asian immigration in the 1980s. Australians have also worried at times about immigrants taking their jobs. Though some racism

Vietnamese immigrants harvesting grapes. Many immigrants come to Australia to find work.

WHERE IMMIGRANTS HAVE COME FROM			
1947		**1991**	
G. Britain & Ireland	73%	G. Britain & Ireland	13%
Rest of Europe	15%	Rest of Europe	13%
Asia	3%	Asia	50%
Other	9%	Other	24%
Source: "Australia in Focus," *Understanding Global Issues*, 1993			

"I'm really happy I'm in this country. First of all, it's really good because I've learned so many new things, like the way of life of people from other countries. We sure have a lucky country. It's still one of the quietest and most peaceful. It's a comfortable life."
—Niki, an immigrant from Greece

does exist in Australian society, it is definitely not the predominant attitude toward immigrants. Most Australians appreciate what immigrants have done for Australia. They have brought new skills that have helped to develop the economy and the arts. Their different cultures have made the country a more interesting place in which to live.

An increasing number of immigrants who come to Australia return to their own country. About 20 percent of immigrants who arrived between 1947 and 1983 have returned. Some are unable to find good jobs in Australia, while others want to be closer to their families. Some immigrants suffer severe disadvantages. They may have lower paid jobs with poor conditions and higher levels of unemployment. These are usually people from non-English-speaking backgrounds.

"I admire the Australian tolerance of people with a different background. The majority accept differences in people. Some demand that you conform to their ways, but in general the people are quite friendly and good although people regard me as a foreigner, not as an Australian."
—**David, an immigrant from Vietnam**

Australian schools are now full of children from different cultural backgrounds.

IMMIGRATION POLICY

Australia accepted many immigrants after World War II because it needed more workers to develop its industries. It also wanted to help refugees who had nowhere else to go. Since 1945, 470,000 refugees have settled in Australia. By the 1970s, it was no longer necessary to increase the population for industry. Today, Australia still takes refugees from all over the world, and it has a family reunion policy, allowing immigrants' relatives to join them in Australia. In recent years, when unemployment has been high, the government has tried to encourage people with special skills and money for business to come to Australia.

From 1901 to 1966, Australia had an unofficial policy called the White Australia policy. This meant that the country only

Above *In the 1950s, people who wanted to emigrate to Australia went to offices like this one in Great Britain to get more information.*

Right *Chinatown in Sydney. Immigrants have brought their different cultures to Australia, making the cities very colorful and interesting places to live.*

allowed immigrants who were white. Australia's plans for future development did not allow for nonwhite immigrants. Countries in Asia and Africa resented this racist policy. Australia abolished it officially by act of Parliament in 1973 and began to take immigrants from countries in Asia.

The immigrants who came to Australia after 1945 were expected to fit into the Australian lifestyle. In the 1970s, governments began to encourage new settlers to maintain their own culture and languages. They also expected the population as a whole to learn about other cultures in Australia. This is official government policy today and is known as multiculturalism.

"We like to think that we might have in our modern nationhood at least some of the elements of a twenty-first century model— diversity, tolerance, openness, and worldliness within the boundaries of national purpose and cohesion."
—Prime Minister Keating speaking on multiculturalism at the Global Cultural Diversity Conference in Sydney, April 1995

 # Cities

Australia is one of the most urbanized countries in the world. Some 86 percent of the population lives on just one percent of the land, mostly in or around cities on the coast. The majority of people live in the state capitals of Brisbane, Adelaide, Sydney, Melbourne, Hobart, and Perth. In addition to its states, Australia has two territories, the Northern Territory, whose capital is Darwin, and the Australian Capital Territory, which is home to the national capital, Canberra.

As all the states developed largely independent of each other in the nineteenth century, their respective capital cities have different histories and features. Visitors to the different capitals today notice that state loyalties are still strong. State rules and laws still differ in areas such as high

People taking part in one of Sydney's many festivals

school education and road laws. Most Australians read newspapers that are produced for sale in their own state. There are only two national daily newspapers, the *Australian* and the *Australian Financial Review.*

The huge distances between cities and their different populations also help explain some of the differences between them. Perth on the west coast of Australia, for instance, has had fewer immigrants from continental Europe or Asia, but many from the British Isles. Melbourne, 2,121 miles away in the southeast corner of Australia, is home to large numbers of immigrants from continental Europe. Melbourne has the biggest Greek population outside Greece.

SUBURBAN LIVING

Most Australians live in the suburbs rather than in or near the city centers. The pattern of cities' growth is more like many American cities than European ones.

Suburbs continue to spread outward from each city's center. In the large cities of Sydney and Melbourne this means that many residents can live more than 30 miles from their city centers.

On the one hand, suburban spread enables Australians to continue to enjoy living in spacious homes with large gardens. On the other hand, it creates problems. Public transportation cannot always meet the needs of those living in outer suburbs, increasing peoples' reliance on cars. The building of services such as schools and stores sometimes lags behind the spread of houses. Other problems, such as rising living costs and an inadequate waste disposal service, add to some of the planners' concerns about the future of Australian cities.

An aerial view of Melbourne's suburbs. All the main cities in Australia have spread into the surrounding countryside during the last 40 years.

"You do not have to be a mindless conformist to choose suburban life. It reconciles access to work and city with private, adaptable, self-expressive living spaces at home. Plenty of adults love that living space and subdivide it ingeniously. For children, it really has no rivals."
—Hugh Stretton, quoted in Australians: From 1939, 1987

Southeast Queensland

Southeast Queensland is Australia's fastest growing region. New residents, especially from other Australian states, are attracted by the sunshine and beaches. At its current rate of growth its urban population may pass Melbourne's before the year 2050.

Planners have not been able to keep pace with the rapid development of the coastline in both directions from the Queensland capital, Brisbane. The results include major traffic jams, high levels of air pollution, and threats to the native environments of koalas. Much money needs to be spent on roads, sewers, power, and water. And amid the attractive townhouses are large pockets of unemployed young people.

Southeast Queensland, according to one Australian commentator, is in danger of being "loved to death."

The Gold Coast

CANBERRA

Canberra is Australia's capital city, although with only 300,000 people it is not Australia's biggest city. Canberra was created to be the capital in 1927, largely as a result of the rivalry between the two most powerful cities, Melbourne and Sydney, at the time of Australia's federation.

Politicians avoided what would have been an explosive reaction from one of the two cities by agreeing to build a national capital roughly halfway between the two. (In fact, Canberra is much closer to Sydney than to Melbourne.)

Until 1927, while Canberra was being built, the federal parliament met in Melbourne. Then it shifted to Canberra, which, for some time, was little more than a small country settlement for public service departments and a parliament. Canberra has grown quickly since World War II and is Australia's largest inland city. It is now both an administrative and political capital as well as a showpiece for tourists. The National Gallery, the Australian War Memorial, and the new Parliament House, opened in 1988, are among the attractions for visitors.

Right *The botanical gardens in Melbourne, one of the city's beautiful attractions*

A seafood restaurant in Sydney. There is a lot to see and do in Sydney and plenty of restaurants from which to choose.

SYDNEY AND MELBOURNE

Sydney and Melbourne comprise about 40 percent of Australia's population. Sydney is Australia's biggest city, with a population of 3.7 million people. It is also one of Australia's most attractive cities, with its beautiful natural setting on Sydney Harbor, and the spectacular architecture of the Opera House and Harbor Bridge.

Sydney attracts more migrants, visitors, businesses, and investors than other Australian cities. In recent years, a number of multinational companies, such as American Express and IBM, have decided to set up their Asia-Pacific headquarters in Sydney. Other Australian cities have not been able to sell themselves as a gateway to the Asia-Pacific economies in the same way. Most Australians are aware of the strong pull of Sydney for people and business. With much of Australia's media concentrated in Sydney, and with the 2000 Olympic Games being held there, the city's high profile seems set to continue.

"Where else in the world could you begin the day with a ride on an Edwardian merry-go-round; eat Balkan food for lunch; stroll through landscaped public gardens or an aviary full of tropical butterflies; eat Himalayan food for dinner; then finish the day with a swim in the moonlit sea? In no other city but Melbourne, recognized by the Americas' Population Crisis Committee, 1990, as the world's most livable city."—**Jane Freeman,** *Melbourne,* ***Australia's International City,*** **1992**

With 3.2 million people, Melbourne is Australia's second largest city. Its golden era was the 30 years following the gold rush of the mid-nineteenth century, when people and money poured into the city.

For much of the twentieth century, Melbourne has been a center for Australian finance. Despite a shift in some of this activity toward Sydney, it remains an important finance and business center. It also enjoys a reputation for its gardens, culture, cosmopolitan atmosphere, and life style.

Harvests of Land and Sea

AGRICULTURE

Australia is the largest exporter of wool in the world and also one of the biggest producers of food. Farms produce enough food and wool to meet the needs of the population and 35 million people overseas. Almost two-thirds of the country is used for growing wheat and grazing sheep and cattle. Some of these farms are well over two million acres in size. Farms in more fertile areas tend not to be as big as this; some are only two acres in size. Despite the size of many farms, 90 percent are family owned and managed. Other goods produced and exported include dairy products, sugar, fruits, cotton, rice, and grains.

This farmer and his sheep are helping to provide one of Australia's biggest exports, wool.

Farming in Australia is a difficult job. There are often droughts and occasionally bad floods. The soil in many parts of the country is shallow and lacking in nutrients. Farmers in Australia have overcome some of these problems through technology and research. Large areas in the southeast corner of Australia were irrigated in the 1870s to improve the supply of water, and fertilizers were used to improve the soil. Although these were at first successful, they caused salt and acid to build up in the soil, which make it difficult to grow anything.

The agricultural industry had to find new customers when Great Britain became part of the European Economic Community (later the European Union, or EU) in 1973. In recent years, the world prices of goods such as wool and wheat have fallen. Farmers have had to change to survive. New labor-saving technology has reduced the number of people employed on farms, but it has made farms more

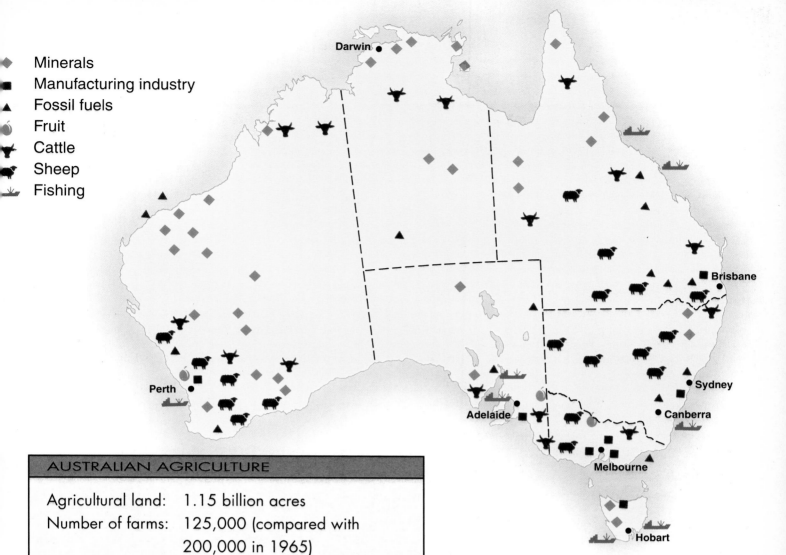

- ◆ Minerals
- ■ Manufacturing industry
- ▲ Fossil fuels
- 🍎 Fruit
- 🐂 Cattle
- 🐑 Sheep
- 🐟 Fishing

AUSTRALIAN AGRICULTURE

Agricultural land: 1.15 billion acres

Number of farms: 125,000 (compared with 200,000 in 1965)

The contribution of agriculture to Australia's Gross Domestic Product has fallen from 20 percent in the 1950s to 4 percent in the 1990s.

Agricultural exports were 75 percent of Australia's export earnings in the 1950s, compared with approximately 25 percent today.

Since the 1950s, the number of farm employees has fallen by 100,000, but the amount produced by farmers has risen by 150 percent.

Agricultural workers make up 5 percent of the working population.

The number of women employed on farms has doubled in recent years.

Source: *The Cambridge Encyclopedia of Australia*, 1994

productive. Farmers are also experimenting with new types of farming, such as cashmere from goats, and tea, coffee, and cocoa.

Asia and the United States are big importers of Australian farm products. Australians are particularly interested in fairer agricultural trade, and they have united with other countries in their region to pursue this goal. One change they would like is fewer restrictions on agricultural imports to the U.S. and the EU.

The Wine Industry

Although grape vines were brought to Australia with the first Europeans in 1788, the international success of the Australian wine industry is fairly recent. Wine exports have been increasing greatly each year. Australian wines are most popular in other English-speaking countries, particularly in Great Britain, and also in Sweden and Japan.

As Australian wines are popular around the world, many countries, especially those in eastern Europe, are seeking advice from Australia's expert winemakers. These experts have become known as the flying winemen because they travel all over Europe to teach people about their methods and technology. French winemakers have also accepted advice from the Australians.

The most famous wine regions in Australia are Barossa Valley, Hunter Valley, Rutherglen, and Margaret River. The Yalumba winery in the Barossa Ranges, South Australia, is Australia's oldest family-owned winery, set up in 1849. It is owned by the Hill Smith family and has survived competition from others by marketing budget priced wines and cask wines (wine that is sold in a box instead of in a bottle). In addition to these, Yalumba produces high-quality red and sparkling wines. Like other Australian wineries, Yalumba now makes wines in Europe. Australian winemakers can travel back and forth between Australian and European summers, producing new wine varieties.

Source: *The Bulletin*, July 26, 1994

Grape pickers in the Barossa Valley, one of Australia's famous wine producing areas

FISHING

Australia's fishing zone is larger than the country itself, but the fishing grounds do not produce as many fish as those in the Northern Hemisphere. However, fishing is a significant industry and provides the income for many coastal towns.

Australia exports the more expensive products from the sea, such as shrimp, lobsters, and pearls. New aquaculture, or fish farming, industries have appeared in recent years, such as shrimp farming—and even crocodile farming.

MINING

In the nineteenth century, gold mining helped Australia's development as a nation. The remote areas of Australia are rich in mineral resources and have made Australia one of the biggest providers of minerals. They account for more than 20 percent of the country's exports. Some of the most valuable exports include iron ore, gold, coal, and bauxite, which is used to make aluminum. Australia is the largest producer in the world of bauxite and aluminum. It is one of the world's largest exporters of iron ore and coal. Uranium is another important export, but the mining of this mineral causes some concern. Uranium is used in nuclear power stations to generate electricity, but nuclear weapons can also be made from uranium. For this reason, the government has allowed only a small amount of uranium to be mined.

Australia sells most of its minerals as raw materials. By not exporting minerals in a more processed form, Australia is badly affected when world mineral prices suddenly fall.

An overhead view of a gold mine, Kalgoorlie. Gold mining remains as important today as it was in the nineteenth century.

31

Forests and Conservation

People protesting the destruction of trees by logging and timber production companies

Australia's native forest area is half the size it was when the settlers arrived. Billions of trees were cut down for timber and to make room for mining and building. Large areas of forest are now within national parks and World Heritage areas, where logging and timber production are not permitted. State forests contain about one-third of the nation's total forested area. In these, timber production and wildlife conservation are managed by government forestry departments. Another third of forest area is privately owned and accounts for half of the country's timber production.

In the 1980s, the concern for the environment grew stronger, and there were many battles between conservationists and timber workers.

Governments have responded to these environmental concerns by making the 1990s a "Decade of Landcare." People now know how important trees are in solving problems like erosion and salinity. A program called Greening Australia has enabled people to plant more than one billion trees.

The major forestry export is eucalyptus woodchips. These are sold to Japan for the papermaking industry. In 1990, 20 percent of wood harvested was from native forests. The rest came from pine plantations, which are expanding. Conservation groups, and a large portion of the population, would like to see logging in all native forests stop completely. This battle for the forests is likely to continue for many years.

Australia's mining industry uses a wide range of advanced technologies, making it very efficient. However, the industry is not without its problems, as people have protested that foreign companies control much of Australia's mining. They have also protested that mining damages local environments. In some areas there is much tension between mining companies and Aborigines regaining title to their traditional lands. This has become an important political issue in Australia.

ENERGY

Homes in Australia generally use electricity and natural gas. The electricity is produced from rich sources of coal. Electricity production is added to by the hydroelectric plants in the Snowy Mountains and Tasmania. In remote areas, there is greater reliance on solar power, which uses the sun to generate electricity. The continent also has a good supply of liquid natural gas. There have been discoveries of light crude oil, and this oil meets 70 percent of the country's needs. It helped to shelter Australia from the effects of increases in the world price of oil in the 1970s. Australia has recently been selling some of its energy to Asian countries, contributing to the rapid expansion of these economies.

Solar energy panels. Solar power is becoming more popular all over Australia, where the sun shines for most of the year in many areas.

Manufacturing and Services

Manufacturing and service industries have become more important to the Australian economy in the last 50 years. They employ the majority of Australian workers. Service industry has grown quickly, particularly in recent years, and accounts for 77 percent of the Gross Domestic Product (the value of all goods and services produced in the year). Although some areas of manufacturing industry have declined, high technology industries have grown. The manufacturing industry is responsible for nearly 15 percent of Australia's Gross Domestic Product.

The ship in the picture above is in front of Sydney's business district. Sydney is home to a vast amount of manufacturing and service industries.

GROSS DOMESTIC PRODUCT	
Services	77 %
Manufacturing	14.5 %
Mining	4.5 %
Farming	4 %
Source: *Australia in Brief*, 1994	

MANUFACTURING

The problem facing manufacturing in Australia is that the country has a very small population for an advanced industrial economy. The distances from other countries and the distances between cities in Australia mean that factories are a long way from their suppliers and customers. This increases transportation costs and makes goods more expensive. For much of this century, in order to assist manufacturers, governments maintained very high tariffs (taxes) on imported goods. In the early 1990s, the government reduced or removed these tariffs to encourage industry in Australia to be more internationally competitive. At first, this severely damaged the car and textile industries, which found it difficult to compete with cheaper labor costs in other countries. The car industry has recovered a little recently, and the manufacturing sector exported 24 percent of its production in 1992, compared with only 14 percent in 1982.

The biggest manufactured export is processed food. New and growing industries are information technology, chemicals and plastics, aerospace technology, scientific and medical equipment, and modern shipbuilding. Australia, however, continues to import a large number of manufactured goods, mostly from the United States and Japan.

Most manufacturing firms are small businesses. The larger firms tend to be foreign-owned and more successful than Australian-owned companies.

Above A traffic jam on Sydney Harbor Bridge. The car industry has picked up recently in Australia, and traffic jams have become a part of life.

Below Cranes are only part of the machinery used in shipbuilding. Modern shipbuilding is a thriving industry in Australian manufacturing.

WORKING CONDITIONS

Australian workers enjoy very good working conditions and a high standard of living. The wages are high and many jobs have particular minimum wages rather than a single minimum wage for every kind of work (so the minimum for carpentry might be higher than for less skilled labor). Working hours are fairly flexible. The average worker works 38 hours per week. Most workers have four weeks vacation every year, and employees in the public sector (people working for the government) have extra vacation time after 10 to 15 years of service. Maternity leave for new parents is also quite generous for public sector workers.

However, this picture is changing. Wages have fallen over the last ten years, as governments have attempted to make businesses more efficient. These attempts have had a number of consequences. The number of part-time positions has increased, and unemployment has risen, though this seems to be gradually improving. The people most affected by unemployment are young people aged 15–19 and migrants from non-English-speaking backgrounds. The government provides special training assistance to these groups to improve their chances of finding a job. Money paid to the unemployed by the government (unemployment benefit) is between 30–70 percent of the average person's wage, depending on whether or not the person has a family.

UNEMPLOYMENT IN AUSTRALIA	
1975	above 5 %
1984–85	8.5 %
1988–89	6.5 %
1993	11.1 %
1995	8–9 %

Source: *The Australian Year Book*, 1995; *The Cambridge Encyclopedia of Australia*, 1994

Marchers protesting taxes at a union-organized demonstration in Sydney.

TRADE UNIONS

Australia has a reputation for being a country with powerful unions. Indeed, Australia was the most unionized country in the world earlier this century, and there were some very big strikes. Unions in Australia still have close links with the Australian Labor Party, the party formed to represent workers.

36

Women in the Workforce

Women at work: a sailmaker (right) and a miner (below).

Over the last decade, the number of Australian women employed has increased by 20 percent. About two-thirds of women between 15 and 64 years old now work. As more women have entered the workforce in greater numbers, changes have been made to improve their working conditions. Equal Employment Opportunity (EEO) laws, introduced in the 1980s, help protect employed women. Governments have also provided more financial assistance for child care for working mothers.

Despite these changes, women's average weekly earnings are still only two-thirds those of men. This is partly because more women work part-time than men. Another reason, though, is that men and women still tend to work in different areas of the workforce, where wages are different. The majority of women have jobs in the service industries, such as stores, offices, schools, and hospitals.

Union membership remained high throughout the 1970s and 1980s. About 55 percent of employees were union members at this time, which was higher than in any other English-speaking country. But union membership has dropped greatly in the 1990s. Only 40 percent of employees are now union members. There are 227 unions in Australia, but this number is also falling as unions are forced, by new rules, to join together.

In recent years, there has been an accord (agreement) between the Australian Council of Trade Unions (the national organization of unions) and the government over wages. This has meant that pay increases have only been given if groups can show improvements in output and efficiency. Since the accord, there have been fewer working days lost because of strike action.

THE SERVICE INDUSTRIES

Almost 80 percent of the Australian workforce now works in the service industries. People who work in the building industry, in stores, schools, banks, and government offices all work in service industries.

The export of services has been increasing over the past few years. The biggest service export is tourism (where tourist services are sold to people visiting Australia). Other service industries that are important exports include international education, computer software, finance and insurance, telecommunications, and transportation. Great Britain has become one of the biggest importers of Australian services.

The majority of Australians work in service industries, like the workers in this bank.

Tourism

Australia's unique wildlife, good climate, contrasting landscapes, and modern cities make it a popular tourist destination. In recent years, the number of international visitors has risen, with more than three million visiting each year. In the 1980s and 1990s, the growth in tourism has created 100,000 new jobs, and tourism now accounts for at least 10 percent of the national income. The most popular places for tourists to visit are the Great Barrier Reef and the Gold Coast in Queensland, central Australia, the Australian Alps, and the capital cities. Unfortunately, tourism can be harmful to the environment. The Great Barrier Reef, for example, is at risk. New building projects and large numbers of visitors cause pollution, which finds its way into the sea, killing coral and sea life. Anchors on tourists' boats also damage the reef. The tourist industry needs to protect those things that people come to see.

Australia has, however, won international awards for tourism projects that are kind to the

The Great Barrier Reef is very popular with tourists. Visitors can choose to see it from above the water or, like this diver, from underwater.

environment. This kind of tourism is called ecotourism. It is even possible for tourists to help improve the environment while on their vacations by working on conservation projects. Volunteers on these projects may plant trees, collect seeds, or record the animals they see.

Daily Life

An Australian family enjoying breakfast before going to work and school

THE FAMILY

On average, Australians marry in their mid- to late-twenties and have two children. As in other modern industrial societies, though, many marriages break up. In 1991, 13 percent of families were single-parent families. There are also more people choosing not to marry, and couples are having children at a later age. For these reasons, larger numbers of people are living alone or are sharing a house with one other person.

HOUSING

Seventy percent of Australians own, or are buying, their homes, usually in the suburbs. The most popular type of house is a single-family brick house, often on a quarter acre of land, with a backyard. Smaller houses or apartments are now being built closer to the cities. These may become more popular as the new suburbs spread farther away from the cities.

OWNERSHIP OF CONSUMER GOODS IN AUSTRALIA	
Car	84 %
Dishwasher	20 %
Refrigerator	99 %
Swimming pool	11 %
Telephone	95 %
Television	97 %
Washing machine	90 %

Sources: *Australia in Brief*, 1994; *The Cambridge Encyclopedia of Australia*, 1994; *The Australian Year Book*, 1995

FOOD

There is an enormous variety of food available in Australia. The cost of food is reasonable, and the quality is very good. The immigrants who have come to Australia have strongly influenced what Australians eat. There are many different types of fruits and vegetables, and specialty shops and market stalls sell foods from all over the world. Australians enjoy eating out, and there are plenty of restaurants from which to choose.

Australians have become more careful about what they eat. Although red meat is still the most popular kind of meat, Australians are eating less of it now than they once did. They now eat more vegetables and twice as much fruit as they did in 1930. Australia's warm climate and outdoor lifestyle make barbecues popular. Australian beer and wine, which are sold all over the world, are popular with Australians as well.

EDUCATION

Most children in Australia begin their schooling with kindergarten. This is a preschool for four year olds and is normally for half a day on weekdays. Children generally begin elementary school at the age of six. They complete seven years of elementary school and then go on to secondary school. It is compulsory to stay in school until the age of 15 (16 in Tasmania), but most students complete the full six years of secondary education. The school day lasts from about 9:00 A.M. until 3:30 P.M.

A special feature of the Australian education system is the large number of students who attend private schools rather than schools run by the government. More than one-quarter of students go to private schools, many of them run by Catholics. A number of private schools, especially non-Catholic schools, charge high fees. They tend to have better facilities than other schools. The government also contributes money to private schools. Some people oppose this because they believe public schools need more money.

Most children in Australia go to private or public schools. Yet some children have to be educated by "schools of the air," using a two-way radio to talk to their teachers, because they live in remote areas where there are few people often living long distances apart.

41

If students do well at secondary school, they can choose to go to a university, an advanced education college, or a technical college. The universities and advanced education colleges have an academic focus, while the technical colleges teach skills for specific jobs such as hairdressing, architecture, or hotel management. Almost half of those aged 15 to 24 attend some sort of educational institution.

TRANSPORTATION

Australia's large size and the spread of the population in the suburbs means that public transportation does not serve everyone well. But there are interesting and innovative ways to travel around the cities and suburbs. In Sydney, for example, people travel by ferry, hydrofoil, and monorail as well as by trains and buses.

Most people still rely on cars. About 84 percent of households have one car. Many have two cars, and more than 10 percent have three cars. The country has half a million miles of roads, and these are used by nine million vehicles.

This ferry in Sydney is used by people to travel to work.

About half of the roads are dirt roads, but the paved National Highway links all the capital cities, where most of the population lives.

Until 1995, it was not possible to travel between some cities on the same railroad because each state had its own rail gauge. Australia now has a standard gauge. Flying between the cities is very expensive, though prices have fallen in recent years.

Sports and Leisure

Even though the majority of Australians live in cities by the coast, they have a fascination and love for the "bush." Each year more than half the population visits the many national parks and World Heritage areas, where people go camping, bush walking, and four-wheel driving.

Because Australians live in suburban houses on large plots of land, they spend a lot of time gardening. On weekends, the sound of the lawnmower is a common one, and large garden centers are filled with people.

Perhaps what many Australians love most, though, is sports. About half the population is involved in organized sports, and others participate in individual sports such as fishing, sailing, surfing, and horseback riding. Australians are enthusiastic spectators of sports. Large crowds gather to see football, cricket, horse racing, and tennis.

There are 130 national sporting organizations and thousands of local sporting clubs. Many different sports are played in Australia, including soccer, football, rugby, cricket, basketball, baseball, and hockey. The most popular sport for women is netball, which is similar to basketball.

Above Pat Cash, a famous Australian tennis player

Below Basketball is popular in Australia.

The Future

Australia's links with Asia will continue to develop in the next century.

Australia continues to change in important ways. Its population, although not growing at the rapid pace it did earlier, continues to become less like the older Anglo-Celtic Australia. It is gradually becoming more Asian. At the same time, Australia's economy is closely tied to the booming economies of eastern Asia. Australian leaders encourage even closer cooperation among the Asia-Pacific countries through organizations such as the Asia-Pacific Economic Cooperation group (APEC).

As changes have been made to the economy, there has been a growing gap between rich and poor. Wages have been kept low and the number of unemployed people has risen. The percentage of workers officially unemployed was below 10 percent in 1995, but there is a lot less security for most workers. Much of the new work is in part-time jobs or jobs contracted for very short periods.

"The story of the 1980s is the attempt to remake the Australian political tradition. This decade saw the collapse of the ideas which Australia had embraced nearly a century before and which had shaped the condition of its people.... Its bedrock ideology was protection; its solution a Fortress Australia, guaranteed as part of an impregnable Empire spanning the globe. This framework—introspective, defensive, dependent—is undergoing an irresistible demolition."—**Paul Kelly (editor of *The Australian* and author), *The End of Certainty*, 1992**

Like other countries, Australia has found it hard to change its economy quickly. Australian governments have urged the people to be patient and to endure the difficult times. The economy has begun to grow in the mid-1990s, which may mean better times ahead for workers.

44

In the 1990s, Australians talk a lot about their new identity. This is sometimes linked to Australia's role in the Asia-Pacific region, sometimes to multiculturalism and the new relationships with Aborigines, and sometimes to a future Australian republic. Often it is a combination of these things. Recent Australian governments have encouraged these discussions, and they are likely to continue toward the year 2000.

By most standards, Australia's economic future is regarded as bright. It is also very different from what most people would have imagined in the 1960s, and it may be some time yet before we can see all the consequences of such rapid recent changes.

AN AUSTRALIAN REPUBLIC

Australia's head of state is Queen Elizabeth II, the queen of England. In 1992, Australia's Prime Minister, Paul Keating, declared that before 2001, Australians would decide whether to become a republic. In 1995, the government revealed its suggested new constitution. A slight majority of Australians have supported the idea of becoming a republic, but the republicans know that they have a lot of work to do yet. Constitutional change is complicated. A proposed change must be supported by both a majority of the people and a majority of the Australian states in order to be successful.

The Sydney Opera House

Glossary

aerospace technology The technology of aviation in Earth's atmosphere and the space beyond it.

Anglo-Celtic Describing people or customs from either England (Anglo) or Ireland, Scotland, and Wales (Celtic).

bushfire A fire that burns wild scrub and forests.

colonies Areas of land settled or conquered and controlled by another country.

conservationists People who support protecting the natural environment.

constitution A collection of rules that set the way a country is governed.

cosmopolitan Combining elements from many parts of the world.

European Economic Community (EEC) Now called the European Union (EU). An association of European states that cooperate closely on economic, social, and political affairs. EU countries do not have economic barriers with one another, but do with outside countries such as Australia.

family reunion Gathering together members of a family who have been separated. Family reunions make up a significant part of Australia's immigration program.

federal government The central government of a union of states.

federation The process of uniting a group of states under a central authority.

fertilizers Materials added to the soil to help make things grow.

Great Artesian Basin The large reservoir of water lying under east-central Australia.

hydroelectric plants Machinery that makes electricity from the power of flowing water.

information technology The technology—including computers—that stores, retrieves, and sends information of all kinds.

irrigation Supplying water to land through pipes and channels.

multiculturalism The encouragement of many different cultures within a society.

munitions Weapons, ammunition, and equipment used mainly for military purposes.

nutrients Substances that nourish growth.

pasture Land used for farming sheep or other livestock.

public sector The part of economic life that is not run by private companies and businesses.

racism The belief that others are inferior because of their race.

rail gauge The distance between the rails on a railroad.

referendum A general vote on a question by the people of a country.

refugees People who have left their home countries because of danger or trouble there.

salinity The level of salt in a substance, such as water or soil.

solar power Energy generated using the sun's rays.

territory Areas forming part of Australia, but not ranked as states.

UNESCO United Nations Educational, Scientific, and Cultural Organization, which helps to educate people all over the world.

urbanization To make an area a town or city, or part of a town or city.

World War I A great European war fought between 1914–1918. The Allies (Great Britain and its empire, France, Russia, and later Italy and the United States) fought and defeated the Central Powers (Germany, Austria-Hungary, and the Ottoman Empire).

World War II A world war fought mostly in Europe and the Pacific between 1939–1945. The Allies (the United States, the Soviet Union, Great Britain, France, Australia, New Zealand, and others) defeated the Axis powers (Germany, Italy, Japan, and others).

Further Information

Further Reading

Australian Aboriginal Culture. Third edition. New York: Australian Government Publishing Company, 1992.

Darien-Smith, Kate and Lowe, David. *The Australian Outback and Its People.* People and Places. New York: Thomson Learning, 1995.

Department of Geography Staff. *Australia in Pictures.* Visual Geography. Minneapolis: Lerner Publications, 1990.

Morris, Scott, ed. *Industry of the World.* New York: Chelsea House, 1993.

Nile, Richard. *Australian Aborigines.* Threatened Cultures. Milwaukee: Raintree Steck-Vaughn, 1992.

Rajendra, Vijeya. *Australia.* Cultures of the World. North Bellmore, NY: Marshall Cavendish, 1991.

Reynolds, J. *Down Under: Vanishing Cultures.* San Diego: Harcourt Brace, 1992.

Addresses

Australian Government Publishing Company, P.O. Box 7, Planetarium Station, New York, NY 10024

The Australian Institute of Aboriginal and Torres Strait Islander Studies, P.O. Box 553, Canberra ACT 2601, Australia

The Australian Tourist Commission, 489 Fifth Avenue, New York, NY 10017

Picture Acknowledgments Maps were provided by Peter Bull. The publishers gratefully acknowledge the permission of the following to use their pictures in this book: Bruce Coleman 14, 18, 37 (bottom); Camera Press Ltd. 16 (bottom), 35 (top); Eye Ubiquitous 4 (top and bottom), 11, 15, 19, 24, 27 (bottom), 28, 32, 33, 34, 38, 42, 43 (top); The Image Bank 8 (top), 9, 16 (top), 17, 25, 35 (bottom); Life File 20, 23, 27 (top), 43 (bottom), Mary Evans 12 (top); Popperfoto 13, 22; Tony Stone *cover, title page, contents page*, 6, 8 (bottom), 10, 26, 30, 31, 39 (top), 45; Wayland 21.

Index

Numbers in **bold** refer to illustrations.

Aborigines 8, **12**, 14, **18**, **19**, 33
Adelaide 8, 24
agriculture 11, 13, **28–29**
Alice Springs 9
ANZUS 16
Asia 14, 17, 20, 23, 44

Bruce, Stanley Melbourne 14
bushfires **8**

Canberra 15, 24, 26
climate **7–8**
Commonwealth of Australia 13, 15
conservation **32**
constitution 45
convicts 13
Cook, Captain James **13**
Cyclone Tracy **7–8**

Darling River 10
desert 9
drought 9

economy 17, 44
education 41–42
energy **33**
European Economic Community (EEC) 28
European settlement 12, 13, 18
Exports 31, 35, 38

family 40
Federal Government 15
federation 14, 15
films 5
fishing 31
food 41
forests **8**, 9, **32**
Franklin River 11
Freeman, Cathy **19**

Gold Coast **4**, **26**, 39
gold rush 13, **14**, 27
Great Artesian Basin 11

Great Barrier Reef 9, 11, **39**
Great Britain 13, 14, 16, 18, 19, 22, 24, 28, 30, 38
Great Dividing Range **10**, **11**
Gross Domestic Product 29, 34

housing 40

immigrants 14, 18, **20–21**, **22–23**
Immigration Policy 22–23
Israel 20

Japan 14, 32, 35

Keating, Paul **15**, 45

Labor Party 15, 36
Liberal Party 15

Mabo judgment 19
manufacturing industries **34–35**
Melbourne 8, 20, 24, **27**
mining **31**, 33
mountains **10**, **16**
multiculturalism 23
Murray River 10, **11**

Native Title Act 19
New South Wales 9, 13, 15, 16
newspapers 24
New Zealand 6, 16
Northern Territory **9**, 24

oil 33
Olgas, the **9**
Olympic Games (A.D. 2000) 5, 27, 45

population 5, 13, 14, 18, 27

Queen of Australia 15, 45
Queensland 9, 13, 26

racism 21, 23

rain forest **8**, 9
refugees 22
religion 42
republic 15, 45

services industry 37, **38**
Snowy Mountains Scheme 16
southern Australia 8
sport 5, **43**
state government 15
suburbs **25**, 43
Sydney 8, 20, **24**, **27**, **34**, **45**

Tasmania 8, 9, 13
terra nullius 19
territories 6
timber 13, 32
Torres Strait Islanders 19
tourism 11, 38, 39
trade unions **36–38**
transport 25, 38, **42**

Uluru (Ayers Rock) **6**, 8, 9
unemployment 21, 22, 36
United States 16, 29, 35

Victoria 9, 13, 16

Western Australia 13
White Australia Policy 22
wine industry 30
women in the workforce 29, **37**
World Heritage **11**, 32, 43
World War I 16
World War II 14, **16**, 18, 22, 26